W9-APL-848

Rumi's Little Book of Life

Rumi's Little Book of Life

The Garden of the Soul, the Heart, and the Spirit

Translated by Maryam Mafi
and Azima Melita Kolin

HAMPTON ROADS

Copyright © 2012 Maryam Mafi and Azima Melita Kolin

All rights reserved. No part of this publication may be reproduced or transmitted
in any form or by any means, electronic or mechanical, including photocopying,
recording, or by any information storage and retrieval system, without permission in
writing from Hampton Roads Publishing, Inc. Reviewers may quote brief passages.

Cover design by Jim Warner
Cover image: Kalenik Hanna © shutterstock.com
Interior designed by Kathryn Sky-Peck

Hampton Roads Publishing Company, Inc.
Charlottesville, VA 22906
Distributed by Red Wheel/Weiser, LLC
www.redwheelweiser.com

Sign up for our newsletter and special offers by going to
www.redwheelweiser.com/newsletter/

ISBN: 978-1-57174-689-4

Library of Congress Cataloging-in-Publication Data available upon request.

Printed in the United States of America
MAL
10 9 8 7 6 5 4 3 2

Foreword

en or so years ago prior to the in-depth discussion of the life and poetry of Rumi that we study as part of the classical Persian poetry course that I teach here at the School of Oriental and African Studies in London, we watched some footage of the whirling dervishes of Konya, as well as scenes of more private gatherings in Turkey and Iran, where Rumi's poetry was either being recited accompanied by music, or crowds of men, crammed in a small hall, were rocking, to and fro, in exuberant states of ecstasy. I was looking at the faces of my predominantly Western European students while they watched the film clips, and I noticed smiles of recognition and expressions of surprise beginning to spread across their faces as they realized that what they were witnessing was not a million miles away from what several, if not most of them, do while dancing in clubs. Eventually, one of the students commented that what he was looking at was just like a small-scale rave, with all the prerequisite ingredients of *peace*, *love*, and *ecstasy*, although, in the case of Rumi-circles, one would assume that the latter state is not chemically induced.

The movement—which started in the 1950s in London and spread across Europe, North America, and Australia, and gradually became a normal group activity for the young in many other parts of the world—encapsulates its credo in four simple words: Peace, Love, Unity, and Respect. Even allowing for variations in the moral and societal vocabulary of different cultures and the evolution of ideas across centuries, these four simple words can equally be described as a distillation of the lessons of Rumi, the 13th century Persian speaking scholar, teacher, and poet.

The intoxicated expressions of love and longing for unity with the immortal Beloved that adorn almost every poem of Rumi, were unleashed after a chance encounter with Shamsoddin of Tabriz in 1244 in Konya, in the Byzantine-ruled lands of Asia minor. Shams was a supreme master dervish who had been searching for years for a highly spiritual companion to whom he could transfer his wisdom. But for those who believe in the games of fate, the coming together of Rumi and Shams was a preordained meeting of an impassioned, mystical teacher and a receptive pupil.

What is it that lies at the heart of the poetry of Rumi that has captivated not only those who can read the 25,000 or more couplets of his *Masnavi*, the 35,000 couplets of his Divan-e Shams lyrical and ecstatic odes, and the more than 2,000 quatrains and fervent prayer-songs of his *Monajat* in the original Persian, but also those beyond the predictable geographical and cultural bounds of Islamic societies, who have come to understand and love him through the translations of selections of his works?

Is it Rumi's lack of censoriousness and dislike of moral Puritanism that have won the hearts of religious as well as secular readers of his poetry, or is it his deep affinity for all stories of separations and trust in the power of love in transforming human destinies?

Mowlana Jalal ad-Din Balkhi-Rumi first honed his understanding of the concept of the divine by immersing himself in the disciplines of theology, philosophy, and law. An industrious student of jurisprudence who devoted his early years to the study of the revelations and traditions of prophets, with apparently little time for poets and their wares, was transformed in his late thirties into one of the most commanding and influential practitioners of poetry, to the extent that his fame is no longer limited to his homeland and he has become one of the best selling poets of stature in North America.

The West's fascination with Rumi, however, did not start in the 20th century in the United States. Some of the oldest translations of Rumi's poetry date back to 1772, when Sir William Jones, the English philologist, translated the opening lines of Rumi's *Masnavi*, or the *Spiritual Couples*:

> *Hear, how yon reed in sadly pleasing tales*
> *Departed bliss and present woe bewails!*
>
> *'With me, from native banks untimely torn,*
> *Love-warbling youths and soft-ey'd virgins mourn.*

O! Let the heart, by fatal absence rent,
Feel what I sing, and bleed when I lament:

Who roams in exile from his parent bow'r,
Pants to return, and chides each ling'ring hour.

My notes, in circles of the grave and gay,
Have, hail'd the rising, cheer'd the closing day.

Currently there are more than several hundred titles that offer English translations of selections of poems of Rumi. These translations appear in every conceivable format, ranging from literal to English rhyme, poetic prose, and metrical renditions. Interestingly, the most favored of these translations, if the sale of the books is any guide to go by, have been the poetic interpretations of the original. Many of the most popular poems of Rumi have been translated by a number of writers, poets, and academics, and although most have remained faithful to the core message of the poem as it attempts to fathom and alleviate man's emotional and spiritual predicament, each attempt is different in terms of form and vernacular.

Hafez of Shiraz (1325–1389) wrote that

Love's sorrow is no more than just one story and yet,
amazingly, it is never the same from whoever I hear it.

Some translators of Rumi have been more successful than others in allowing the reader a more rewarding and informative introduction to his poetry. But what do we expect from translators who, more often than not, have to grapple with the complexities of the semantic content of the original verse, as well as transfer the notorious word plays possible in the Persian language into their language of translation? Some of the challenges would be enough to persuade any translator to omit the untranslatable. But a successful translator should be able to capture the "spirit" and the "soul" of the poem. In 1791, when Sir William Jones was translating classical Persian poetry, Frances Tyler emphasized in his *Principles of Translation*, the first systematic study in English of the translation process, that the most important fact is that "the translation should have all the ease of the original composition." Furthermore, one could add to Tyler's simple idea that the sacrosanct status of the original poem should in no way prevent the poetic translator from bringing her own interpretation of the poem into the translated version, and depending on her own creativity, she could replicate the play with words, form, meter, and rhyme, as long as the translation flowed and did not stumble as it was received by a new audience.

The translator must anticipate that the poem in its new robes of the foreign language will be read by a whole host of readers, ranging from those who are perhaps familiar with the original text and know much about the period and circumstance of the writing of the original, to those who may know very little indeed; they may not only know little about the original poem but even less about the stringent literary structures of classical Persian poetry and the mandate that poetic utterances cannot be delivered outside the confines of meter and rhyme. The translator must decide whether she should retain an *accent* in the translation, and by doing so, bring the original poet into the home and hearts of the American or English reader. On the other hand would it be better if the translator were to organize a foreign tour and take the readers on an exotic, adventurous journey to the home, the era, and the world of the Persian speaking poet?

I think Maryam Mafi and Melita Kolin's lucid, poignant, and beautiful translation of Rumi poetry have managed to fulfil all the expectations of the newcomer, the curious, and the old devotee of Rumi's poetry and teaching by being a guide through the topography of Rumi's writing and by preparing us to host him in our homes and our hearts.

The rapture that burns quietly through much of Rumi's poetry comes through in their translations as they captivate our imagination and let us into the inner sanctum of Rumi's passionate and joyful spirituality. In their translations, we understand that Rumi's God is not in the mosque, the monastery, or the fire-temple, but resides in the House of Intoxication, built in a lush Garden of Illumination, where a ladder of love leads to the divine. We learn that Rumi's God is not there to punish but is there to love and to rescue the Soul, the Heart, and the Spirit. The only "right commanded" by Rumi is that the mirror of the heart be polished of tarnish and the only "wrong forbidden" by him is that love should ever be conditional.

Friends, let us return to the source of pure essence
that nothing else can equal. Remember,
we are pearls in the ocean of spirit, if not, why are
these constant waves surging through our hearts?
The primeval wave created the vessel of this body,
as it breaks we will be united with the Friend.

The late Shusha Guppy (December 24, 1935, Tehran, Iran–March 21, 2008, London, UK) writer, singer, and erudite Rumi commentator, recorded a cover version of a song by Leonard Cohen's that she loved and was certain was inspired by Rumi. The 1971 song, *Joan of Arc*, contains these words:

It was deep into his fiery heart
he took the dust of Joan of Arc,
and then she clearly understood
if he was fire, oh then she must be wood.

—Narguess Farzad
Senior Fellow in Persian,
School of Oriental & African Studies
London

Part One

Garden of the Soul

Come back my soul, how much longer
will you linger in the garden of deceit?
I have sent you a hundred messages
I have shown you a hundred ways
either you never read them
or you ignore my advice.
Come back my soul, do not waste
time with the cold-hearted
they do not know your worth.
Why do you seek water
when you are the stream?
Have you forgotten? You are
the king's falcon, you are a ray
of the Beloved, a divine wonder!

Indulging our pride, we run after
every fleeting image.
How odd that being so unimportant
we cultivate such grand illusions.

Do not grieve over past joys, be sure
they will reappear in another form.
A child's joy is in milk and nursing
but once weaned, it finds new joy
in bread and honey.
Joy appears in many different forms
it moves from place to place.
It may suddenly show in the falling rain
or in the rose bed; it comes now as water,
now as beauty, or as nourishing bread.
But suddenly it may show its face
from behind the veil and destroy all idols
that prevent you from seeking the divine.
In sleep when the soul leaves the body
you may dream of yourself as a tall cypress
or as a beautiful rose, but be warned, my friend,
all these phantoms dissolve into thin air
once the soul returns to the body.
Do not rely on anything but your heart.

Man may tolerate the rain for awhile
but soon he looks for shelter
while ducks quack happily for
rainwater is their sustenance.

The intellect is luminous and seeks justice
so why does the dark ego prevail over it?
Because the ego is at home in the body
while the intellect is only a visitor,
the ego-dog at his own door is like a lion.

If one were to tell an unborn child that
outside the womb there is a glorious world
with green fields and lush gardens
high mountains and vast seas, with a sky
lit by the sun and the moon, the unborn
would not believe such absurdity.
Still in the dark womb how could he imagine
the indescribable majesty of this world?
In the same way, when the mystics speak of worlds
beyond scent and color, the common man
deafened by greed and blinded by self-interest
cannot grasp their reality.

Having built a hen house for yourself
do not invite a camel in!
The hen house is your body,
the hen is your intellect, and the camel
is Love's majesty in all its glory.

The five senses are linked together
for all five have grown from the same root,
when one is strengthened, the rest are enhanced.
Seeing enhances speech, communication
increases vision, and sight stimulates and
awakens every sense to spiritual perception.
If one sense breaks free from its bonds
having a glimpse of the invisible
it makes it apparent to all the others.
You have seen how when one sheep jumps
over the creek the whole flock follows.
So drive the flock of your senses to pasture
and let them graze on the heavenly flowers
in the Garden of Truth.

"Tell me," my lover asked me tenderly,
"how could you live without me?"
I said, "without you I am lost
like a fish out of water."
He smiled, "This is only your own fault."

Suddenly my Guest appeared.
Startled, my heart asked, "Who is there?"
"The glorious moon," answered my soul.
The Guest was in the house but we, like lunatics,
were running in the streets searching for him.
"I am here!" he kept calling from inside
while we like doves kept cooing,
"Where, where are you?"
As when a crowd gathers in the night shouting
"Help, help there is a thief!" and the thief
who is among them also keeps shouting,
his cries mixed with and drowned by the crowd.

The saying, "He is with you," means
in your search for Him, He is with you,
closer to you than yourself, why seek outside?
Melt like snow, wash yourself from yourself,
and let love grow in your soul, silent as a lily.

Only ignorance keeps a bird encaged.
The Masters have fled from their cage
and have become guides, showing that
the only way out of ignorance is faith.

You have the habit of walking slowly
holding grudges and resentments.
Ill-tempered and greedy, small-minded,
and with so many attachments
how do you expect to attain union?
Leave this muddy water and seek clarity.
Being so weak, you need all the help
and the grace of God to overcome
the waves and reach the shore to safety.
Take shelter with those who need no shelter.
Only on the horse of love can you go beyond
the sun and moon to behold the Perfect One.

Questioning cannot unravel the secret of truth
nor giving away your wealth and position.
Mere words do not exalt the heart
pain is the price that the heart has to pay.

You may be proud and conceited but
you cannot impress the sun by flirting.
Stop walking in your own shadow
wallowing in your foolish thoughts.
Raise your head, look at the sun, walk
among the flowers, become a human being.
Do not dwell in darkness like a night bird
prey for the monsters of your imagination.
Get up and seek the light, look toward the sun.

This body is a guesthouse
each morning someone new arrives.
Welcome them all for they may be
messengers from the invisible.
Do not feel burdened by them
or they may go back to non-existence.
Each time a thought enters your heart
treat it as an honored guest, your worth
is shown by the thoughts you entertain.
Embrace sorrowful thoughts for they
sweep the house of your heart clean,
scatter the withered leaves, and pull out
the twisted roots, preparing the ground
for the new shoots of joy.
What sorrow takes away from the heart
it replaces with something better.
Without the fury of thunder and lightning
the plants will be scorched by the sun.
Be grateful for all you receive,
good and bad alike, for it may be a gift
from the treasury of Spirit that will bring
the fulfillment of your most secret desire.

I wish that grief and sorrow would
shatter your heart, disloyal lover,
and deprive you of everything
you value in the world.
As no one remembers me but sorrow
I bless it a thousand times a day.

Greetings from your drunken lover!
You stole my heart, Beloved,
now I am offering my life.
Friends, let Him intoxicate you completely
for being half drunk is of no use.
His wine is like an electric spark for the soul.
There are many pale faces in Love's kingdom
much sorrow and many tears, but do not fear
for your reputation. Once you become
an empty cup the Wine-Bearer
will fill you with Divine Love.
Fear not for your reputation
you will be glorified.

God has given us wine so potent that those
intoxicated with it escape from the two worlds.
He has put into the form of hashish, a power that
delivers the one who tastes it from self-consciousness.
He has made sleep so it erases every thought.
God has created thousands of wines that can take over
our minds. Do not be deceived by every kind of wine!
Jesus was intoxicated with God; his donkey, with barley.
Seek the wine of joy from the blessed ones
in whom it is stored.
Every object of love is like a jar, one full with dregs
another full of pure pearls.
Any wine will get you high, but be a connoisseur
and taste with caution, judge like a king and choose
the one not tainted with fear and vain expectations.

The mouse-soul is a nibbler and has been
given a mind proportionate to its needs.
The Almighty gives nothing without need.
God would not have created the earth if
the world did not need it. If the earth did not
need mountains, He would not have made them
so majestic. If there was no need for the sun,
the moon, and the stars, He would not
have created them. He has given man tools
according to his needs. Need, then,
is the cause of all things in existence, so
increase your need quickly so the sea
of His benevolence may surge in generosity.

What is this hurricane blowing from heaven
making thousands of ships stagger and sway like drunks?
It is by wind that ships sail and by wind that they sink.
God commands the winds as we command
our breath when we blame or praise.
Different winds blow from the invisible
some bring blessings, others devastation.
The wind is apparent but the source is hidden.
The pure of heart perceive the source and
are guided by its light. Their faith unshakable
they keep silent, their eyes firm on the path
collecting wisdom. Those blind to the source
become form-worshipers, gambling their life.
They sit at the feet of great masters
repeating their words, fussing over faith,
looking for smoke as proof of fire.
Be like the Sun, King without courtiers,
silent and still as a fulcrum.

Do not be fooled, my friend,
this world is not to be trusted.
It will intoxicate you with its
sweet drink and suddenly
desert you and wrap its arms
around another lover.

Flowers live for a short moment, but the flowers
that grow from reason remain fresh.
The blossoms of earth wither and fade
the blossoms of the heart, what a joy!
We delight in all known sciences, but they are
only a small bunch from God's Garden.
We hold on to these few bunches because
we have shut ourselves out of the Garden.
Unless you become a lover of God
you are an echo, a mountain with no voice of its own.
The echo is a reflection from another source
like your speech and feelings.
Speech not inspired by the Divine
springs from self-will and floats like dust
in the air, like moths in the sunbeam.

The senses are the tools of the mind
and the mind is the tool of the Spirit.
When the mind becomes confused, it is
Spirit that brings back clarity and harmony.
Our desires and thoughts spread over the soul
as weeds spread over the surface of a pond.
The ego thrives in muddy water while
the mind needs clarity and transparency.
Let the mind become the master
and the senses, its obedient servants.
A master who puts his senses to sleep is able
to perceive the unseen emerging from Spirit.
Even in his waking state he dreams,
dreams that open the gates to Divine Truth.

I wash my heart of all knowledge and forget myself
for I cannot stand before the Beloved believing
to be a master of all arts. I am only a shell for Spirit.
I leave reason behind and leap into bewilderment.

The assembly of lovers is like fire,
you are like water that puts out the fire.
The sun shines upon this gathering; leave,
for you are a cloud blocking the sun.
Sit not at the table of lovers, you are still
raw and uncooked. Yet you rush ahead
on your wooden horse to danger but
the Gatekeeper knows where you belong.
Choose love, my friend, which is cash in hand
or self-restraint if you are after reward.
Sit with those who are awake or the caravan
will leave while you are still asleep.

Once you express your sorrow
from the bottom of your heart
it will be washed away.
Look at a flower
it can never hide its scent nor its color.

Man is hidden behind his words
his tongue is a curtain over the door of his soul.
When a gust of wind lifts the curtain
the secret of the interior is exposed,
you can see if there is gold or snakes
pearls or scorpions hidden inside.
Thoughtless speech spills easily out of man
while the wise ones keep silent.
Faulty eyes see the moon double and that
gazing in perplexity is like a question;
once you connect with Divine Light
the question and the answer become one.
But if you only hear the answer, do not be fooled
for the ear is simply a go-between.
While the eye perceives reality directly
the ear relies on the promise of words.
From words alone you cannot know fire
do not rely on knowledge derived from others
there is no certainty until you burn.
Make the ear sharp so it becomes an eye
if not, words become entangled in the ear
and the truth can never reach the heart.

The Light that is life to the wise
the eyes of the weak cannot endure.
The fire for melting iron is not suitable
for cooking apples, they need a gentle heat.
But these flames are too gentle for a dervish,
who, like the iron, draws willingly that fiery heat
onto himself. Bearing hardship, happy and red,
he goes straight into the heart of the flames
setting his whole being ablaze.
He is the heart of the world, for the theater
of God's action is not the body but the heart.

To dance is not to jump to your feet
and rise painlessly in the air like dust.
To rise above both worlds is to dance in
the blood of your pain and give up your life.

All excitement comes from the cup of wine
the Beloved spilled upon this earth.
His fragrance makes you drunk with ecstasy
His light bewilders the heart.
If your heart is heavy you must be
only in love with yourself.
Turn your gaze toward Him and
He will heal you! His breath will blow away
the autumn winds of denial and cover
the thorns in the garden of your heart
with His blossoms.

There are two intellects!
One is acquired from teachers and books,
from repetition and sciences, granting a sense of superiority
yet the effort to sustain it becomes a great burden.
It ends just as the water supply coming from outside
a house stops once the source has dried up.
The other intellect is God's gift.
With a fountainhead in the heart of Spirit
the water of knowledge bubbling from within
can never become stagnant or old.
Seek that fountain within yourself!

Clergy knowledge is based on religious law
the knowledge of judges is based on proof
but the knowledge of the divine messengers
is based on direct perception of the Light of God.

The degrees of human intelligence
extend from earth to heaven
some are bright as the sun
others as dim as a distant star.
Some are like a flickering lamp
others like a bolt of fire.
The small mind is a disgrace to
the Universal Intelligence for
worldly desires deprive man
from knowing the Truth.
But there is a superior kind of intelligence
free from the clouds of desire
that can behold the Light of God.

Let the dust under your feet
settle on my eyelashes.
When you torment me, I rejoice
for it is a sign of your loyalty.

When everyone has fallen asleep and
the house is empty and still, it is time
to enter the garden, pull the skirt
of the apple closer to the peach, and
whisper the rose's secret to the jasmine.
Spring, like Christ, murmurs spells that
bring back to life the martyred plants.
They open their lips in gratitude and the soul
becomes intoxicated with their fragrance.
From the glow emanating in the darkness
from the face of the rose and the tulip
I can see the hidden light within them.
A leaf quivers on a branch and my heart trembles
the wind stirs the leaves and beauty stirs my heart.

"Give up the known, give up your life
for the mystery of Love's eternal wine."
"But before I die," I said, "I would like to know you."
"Once you know me there will be no more dying."

Oh gardener, gardener
autumn has come
how desolate is every branch and leaf.
Oh gardener
can you hear the trees' lament
standing leafless in rows
mourners dressed in black, weeping?

No tears come without reason
no face is pale without an aching heart.
The black raven of sorrow has entered the garden
stamping his feet upon the withered green,
"Where is the rose bed now, where are the lilies,
the sweet jasmine and cypress?
Where are the fruit trees, the green grasses,
the nightingale, and the glorious peacock?"

Like Adam, expelled from paradise
all trees are stripped of their robes and crowns
and the garden, frozen in lament, lies waiting
for the Lord's promise of hope.

continued

But you, blasphemous raven, wait!
To your envy the ice will melt,
the water will flow again in the streams,
and colors and scent will return.

The trumpet of resurrection will restore life to the world
filling the rose garden with laughter
and the nightingale's song.
Autumn will die and we will dance upon its grave.
Rejoice, for the dawn of Splendor is breaking!

I have died a hundred times, Beloved,
yet Your fragrance brought me back.
I have lost my soul a hundred times
yet Your voice brings it back.
The vow we made in that glorious hour
You kept; I broke it a hundred times
tricked by my desire to reach You.
How I long to set my eyes on You again
and offer my heart as bait for Your love.
You are the flame burning in the hearts of men
circling like the moon around the azure dome of my heart.

One early morning in the garden I picked a flower
the Gardener suddenly appeared and I panicked.
"Why worry about a flower, when I have
given you the entire Garden!"

Precious soul, do not delay
embark on the wondrous journey
to the sea of meaning!
Remember, you have passed through many stages
do not resist, surrender to the journey.
Wash your wings from the earth's clay
and follow the trail of those before you.
Do not linger in the potter's shop
break the jug and flow with the stream of life.
Rush down from the mountain to the sea
for the mountain offers no refuge.
Do not wander east or west
aim straight at the sun!
From its light, like the moon,
you will sometimes be a crescent
and sometimes full.

In the first stage man is only a form
then Spirit brings the beauty of disposition.
In the first stage fruit is only a form
then comes its delicious taste, which is its purpose.
First beautify yourself, then invite the Beloved as a guest.

Unable to reach Your lips, Beloved,
I keep kissing jeweled hands.
Unable to reach Your sky, Beloved,
I keep prostrating on the ground.

Ask God for love not for life
ask God for soul food not for bread.
The world of created beings is like
pure transparent water in which
shine the attributes of God.
Knowledge, justice, mercy
reflect in that water as the stars of heaven.
Generations upon generations pass, yet
the moon is the same. Times and people change
but the essence of wisdom and justice is the same.
The beautiful ones mirror God's Beauty
and to love beauty is to love Him.

The signs of drying up resemble a branch
that cannot bend or sway.
The limbs of those detached from the world
are supple like a fresh branch that bends
easily in the weaving of a basket.
Many are those whose concepts and fantasies
have drained them of the sap of life
unable to bend or sway in any direction.
My words may be symbolic but they are like fire.
Have you seen how quickly dry branches burn?
There is no protection from the fire of Spirit.
Everything perishes except His Face.
Empty yourself of yourself and contemplate
the words that spring from the silence of God.

Dear soul, spring breeze is here
go into the rose garden and listen
to the whispers of the grass,
the lily, and the hyacinth,
"What you have sown you shall reap."
Look how after the devastating winter
the new blossoms have covered the thorns,
look how tall the cypress has risen in glory.
Spirit and water have graced the rose garden
enhancing its beauty.
What a blessed companionship!
How long will your heart
stay imprisoned in the winter of lust?
Ask the heart for the way, ask the soul for the moon.
Rise and wash your face with the same water
that made the face of the rose so beautiful.

Taste the joy of true faith
and the temptations of the world will fade.
But from a brain so easily tippled expect little.
Sell your brain and buy bewilderment!
Such an exchange will bring you a great profit.

Your mind can fly to great heights
but your parrot-nature keeps pecking on the ground
collecting knowledge that burdens the soul.
Unlearn everything and embrace madness!
Give your profit to the poor, forsake security,
live dangerously, insult those who praise you,
drink poison, and spill the water of life.
Forget reputation, become a disgrace.
I was prudent all my life
from now on, I embrace madness.

Proud scholar
step down from your summit
fall in love and become a fool!
Become humble like dust
walk with everyone
good and bad, young and old
so one day
you may become a king.

You carry a basket full of bread, yet
you beg for crumbs from door to door.
You are up to your knees in water, yet
you beg for a drink from everyone you see.
Why are you so blind and stubborn?
Beg at the door of your heart instead.

Thousands of fools pay gold to the devil
unaware that what they buy is only pain.
The Tailor of Time does not make clothes
without cutting the cloth first.
Beautiful flowers feast the eyes yet
eating them will make you sick.
You hold a corpse in your arms
unaware that it will freeze your body and soul.
You throw the dice of time recklessly
unaware that your opponent is the Master of backgammon.
You stretch your legs comfortably
on the sweet bed of this earth
unaware that it is only borrowed.
In the midst of the dust lift your eyes to Spirit
and speak without words like the angels
whispering from the lapis lazuli roof of the world.

You may be pious, indulging in your prayers
but hurry, for home is far away.
You may think you are spiritual
indulging in ecstasy
but a hundred caravans have passed you by
and you are still fast asleep.

Love is my religion!
Living only in the mind and body
is a disgrace for me.
Love has swept the dust from my soul
and now in the clear sky
my spirit moon is shinning.
For ages I have been beating
the drum of love for you to the tune of,
My life depends on my dying.

Threaten not the selfless
with the sword of anger
you will only harm yourself.
They have found safety in selflessness
mirroring all that is around them.
Spit at that mirror, you will be spitting at yourself.
What you see, ugliness or beauty,
is your own reflection.
Simple and pure
the selfless act as a mirror for the world.

~

Heart, be considerate
soul, be tolerant
patience, run if you cannot bear grief
reason, go and play your childish games.

All selfish pleasures are fleeting and deceitful
as a flash of lightening followed by darkness.
By that light you can neither read nor reach your destination.
Your road will be long and without a guide,
deception will drag you mile after mile
at night into the wilderness.
One moment you stumble against a mountain
the next you fall into a river.
Because of your fascination with lightening
the beams of sunrise have withdrawn from you.
You may journey far
led only by opinion as insubstantial as lightening.
But opinion cannot replace the truth
the lightening flash has blinded you to the rising sun.
Come and climb to our boat
or at least tie your boat to ours.

In the Garden of Love you cannot relax
even for a moment or you will lose
your place in the lovers' queue.
Be sharp as a thorn if you want
the Beloved to sit beside you.

If you are narrow minded
the whole world will appear narrow to you.
If you are happy and with friends
the world will seem a garden of roses.
Many have gone as far as Syria and Iraq
and seen nothing but unbelief and hypocrisy.
Many have gone as far as Herat and India
and seen nothing but buying and selling.
Many have gone as far as Turkestan and China
and seen nothing but deceit and trickery.
If the traveler is after external sensations
he may travel the world and see nothing of spirit.
If a cow walked through Baghdad it will see nothing
of the delights of the city but the rind of a melon.
But the spacious realm beyond cause and effect
is the abode of God, ever changing and forever new.
Everything, be it Paradise or the rivers of Eden,
becomes ugly when fixed permanently in one aspect.

Our eyes cannot perceive God
He perceives us.
Form springs from Spirit
as speech rises from thought.
We know not from where the sea of thought
emerges, but if the waves of thought
are noble and pure, we know the sea
they arise from is noble too.
Forms are born from the Word and die again
like waves returning to the sea.
We too, with every instant die and return to Him.
The world renews itself continuously
while appearing to us the same.
Verily unto Him we are returning.

Seeker, when you feel your soul contracting
know it is for your own good
allow not your heart to burn with grief.
In times of expansion you spend
and this expenditure requires
an income of painful soul searching.
If it was always summer, the roots would burn
and the gardens would never become green.
Winter seems bitter but it is also kind.
When contraction comes, my friend,
behold the expansion within
be cheerful, do not complain.
The eyes of a child are fixed on the wants of now
while the eyes of the wise see to the end.
When you close your mouth
another one will open, seeking nourishment
in the mysteries of Spirit.
The sugar of sensual joy
is the fruit of the garden of sorrow
this joy is the wound, the sorrow is the plaster.
Learn to embrace sorrow
look straight at its face and joy will reappear.
All action sways between contraction and expansion
both as important as the opening and closing
of the wings of a bird in flight.

How lonely it is on God's sea
with no shore in sight
and we, like ships in the night,
navigate only by the grace of His Light.

Do you know where you come from?
You come from the divine sanctuary.
Do you not remember passing through
those ecstatic spiritual stages?
Since you have forgotten them
now you feel bewildered and lost.
You have sold your soul for a handful of dust.
What a cheap bargain you have struck!
Give back the dust and recognize your worth
you are not a slave, you are a king.
It is for your sake that the beautiful hidden ones
have descended from heaven.

Welcome sweet melody!
You bring signs from the unseen
you bring life to this dead world.
Bypass the ear and strike my soul
lift it up to the enchanted world
where you have carried my heart.
The joy you bring is proof that
you have had a long sip
of the heavenly wine, your sweetness
is proof that you have tasted
the heavenly nectar.
From the seeds you have sewn
new shoots are beginning to sprout.

Part Two

Garden of the Heart

Only in the vast haven of the heart
filled with fresh springs
with rose garden within rose gardens
can ecstasy be found.

I wonder, restless heart, where do you
come from and what sustains you?
What did you see in the world of non-existence
that pulls you there, rushing breathless,
drunk and broken from the mountain top
to the sea of nothingness?
While every being fears non-existence
you take no advice and cannot be charmed.
What wind has brought you here?
I am devoted to you yet you bar my road to reason
inflicting pain and trying to destroy me.
My heart whispered, "Do not be so concerned,
in the midst of people I am like a gold coin
hidden in the dust, but even gold cannot
find buyers unless it is brought out from
the depths of the mine into the light."

If you have no lover, look for one
if you have, why aren't you rejoicing?
If your lover is not compliant, mirror him
if he is not polite, teach him manners
if he is standing in your way, fight him!
But instead, you sit here idly pondering
over the strangeness of life.
What is strange, my friend, is you
not seeking the beyond.
You are a being of light yet your heart
is shrouded in darkness.
You are gold melting in the furnace
yet you still search for gold.
Have you forgotten you are an old drunkard
familiar with Love's wine?
Make your spirit blind to all but God
beg at night so the radiant moon
hidden in the shadow of your being may rise.
I drink the wine that is the fire of love
from the hand of my Beloved.
Become the wood for the Beloved's fire
your life will not be wasted.

The night is blind to the glory of dawn
man is blind to the glory of the lover.
He who complains of burning is not a lover
for the lover's heart is constantly on fire.

If you are unaware of the infinite hues of Love
in the eyes of God you are no more than a stone.
Only Love can squeeze water out of stone
only Love can clear the rust from the mirror of the heart.
When Love in all its majesty opens its mouth
like a whale it devours everything
it bewilders the mind and overwhelms the soul.
Love is the lion of Truth.
Distrust causes war, trust restores peace
but Love sets fire to both!
Only on the wings of Love can the heart fly
to where the Beloved dwells.

The Friend is your eye, keep it pure
do not stir the dust with the broom of your tongue.
Withdraw from strangers not from friends
a fur coat is for winter not for summer.
When the ego joins with another ego
darkness increases and the path is lost.
When intelligence joins with another
the light increases and the path becomes clear.

My poetry is as Egyptian bread
left overnight it becomes hard and stale,
eat it while it is fresh.
My poetry is as fish on dry land
quivering for a moment yet before long
it becomes cold and lifeless.
If you eat it, imagining it is fresh
what you eat my friend is only your imagination.
My poetry lives only in the warmth of awareness
in the cold of this world it dies.

This world is like a tree
and we as unripe fruit cling upon it
not yet ready for the King's palace.
When the fruit ripens sweet it lets go of the branch.
When one acquires a taste for that other sweetness
the world loses its appeal.
Holding tight to this world is a sign of immaturity.
As long as you are an embryo
blood drinking is your only interest.

You may be dark as iron
but keep polishing your heart
until it becomes like a mirror
reflecting images from the unseen.
Your mind is a polishing instrument
use it until the heart begins to shine.
But instead you have imprisoned
the intellect and freed your senses.
Man is like the water of a river
when turbid, you cannot see
the gems and pearls lying underneath.
Do not stir the water if you want to see
the reflection of the moon and the stars.
The spirit of man is like air, but when the dust
is stirred, the sun becomes obscured.
God has graced you with vision
that can help you find your way to the Light.

Of the rain at night no one is aware
for every soul is asleep.
Yet the freshness of the rose garden in the morning
is evidence of the rain that no one saw.

My heart is an oyster
the face of my Beloved is the pearl.
He has filled the whole space
and left none for me.
I am amazed at those who say
that the truth is bitter
for me it tastes so sweet that even
the lips of the night have opened.
People may look for nourishment outside
but mine comes from within.
If you want to become as light as the angels
to strip from your clothes is not enough.
Undress completely from yourself.

Open your door, Beloved,
You are the wine, I am the cup
You are eternal, I am a prisoner of time.
"Silence fool, who would open his door to a madman?"

A child bitterly cried beside his father's coffin,
"Why are they taking you to such a narrow house,
so dark and cold, with no carpets, no doors,
and no way out!
With no smell of cooking, no kind neighbors,
why are they taking you to such a lonely place?"
A boy walking with his father overheard
the child's lament
and asked, "Father, are they taking the corpse
to our house?"
"Don't be foolish!" His father answered annoyed.

"But everything the child mentioned describes our house
no carpet, no lamp, nor food."
Many pass their lives deprived of love
unaware that their heart is dark and narrow
where the sun never penetrates.
A grave is better than such a heart.

Open the window of your heart
and look at the Beloved's face.
Love's task is to create that window
so His Beauty may illumine the heart.
It is in your power, my friend,
to gaze constantly at the Beloved's face.
Make a way to the core of yourself
and banish all other impressions.
You possess an elixir
apply it and by its alchemy
you will turn your enemies into friends.
Thus perfecting yourself
you will be able to reflect the Beloved
whose Grace is the nourishment of Spirit.

If you do not know me, ask the dark night
she is the witness of my lonely tears and laments
she is the keeper of my secrets.
I have become patient as a mountain, humble like dust.
My sorrows like a fence of thorns surround my garden
but once you go beyond them you will praise
its flowing springs and fragrant roses.
Praise the Beloved who blessed the garden with new life.
A peaceful weaver cannot appreciate the art of war
the mind cannot feel the sweetness of the lover's pain
that sweet pain of melting like a grain of salt
in the sea of love.
But I will not waste my words on tired minds
I only talk to those who are thirsty for the sea.

Losing my Self
I became God's interpreter.
Now, drunk or sober
I barely utter a word.

Cruel autumn has arrived!
The rose's red dress is torn
the willow's branches have dropped
repenting for missed prayers.
The lily has drawn her sword
the jasmine is shielded ready to fight.
The nightingale
jealous of the rose's admirers
suffers in silence.
The trees lifting their arms in despair
wonder why the buds are hidden
and who has broken the violets' back.
Cruel autumn has arrived but behold
the hope of spring for whatever
autumn destroys spring will replenish.
All this talk of roses, nightingales, and gardens
is only a screen I hide behind
because Love is jealous.

Having lost you, Beloved,
spring brings me no joy
may thorns cover the garden
may stones rain.

You came, Beloved, awoke me
from my sleep and vanished.
In my heart you rose as the moon
yet as I glanced at you, you disappeared.
Having had a glimpse of your garden
I no longer have patience to endure my existence.
One sip of your intoxicating wine
has left me lovesick with longing.
Can a house stand when
its foundations have been shaken?
On the path of love many are the highs and lows
many unions and separations.
Oh, how endless seems the journey
to that wondrous place where my passion draws me.

Once a believer asked the angel of the Gate,
"Is it true that hell is the road through which
both believers and unbelievers pass?
For on my way here I saw neither smoke nor fire."
"The road you passed was hell indeed," the angel smiled,
"but since you have overcome your lower nature
to you it appears as a garden.
Having planted the seeds of devotion, you transformed
the fire of anger into compassion and ignorance
into wisdom. The thorns of envy have turned into roses
so now your fiery soul has become a rose garden
where nightingales sing praises."

Carrying your baggage toward silence
search for signs on the path but
do not mistake yourself as one.
Fix your eyes firmly on the friends of the Prophet
they are your guiding stars.
Keep silent, for words only blur your sight.

Gently, gently open your eyes
and look at the face of Love
gaze at her intoxicating eyes!
Let her smiling face lure your heart
into her infinite garden.
Taste the sweetness of her fruit
drink the scent of her roses and dance
swaying like a willow in the wind.
Forsake worldly pleasures
for the deeper fulfillment
of the infinite mystery of Love.

One kiss from my mischievous lover
kindled a thousand raging fires and
left me numb and burning with passion.
Now mad and longing for another kiss
I run faster than my heartbeat.
What could have happened, I wonder,
if he had kissed me six or seven times?

I speak and he commands, "be silent!"
I am silent and he shouts, "speak!"
I am excited and he commands, "calm down!"
I am composed and he shouts,
  "You are not mad enough!"

I became intoxicated and my heart fled from me.
Where did it go?
It saw the chain of reason break and flew immediately.
No good searching the house, it could have flown
only to the sanctuary of the Beloved.
The heart is a bird of the air
the white falcon of the King
it must have flown back to Him.

The body is like a pot with the lid on
lift the lid to see if it is filled
with the Water of Life or the poison of death.
Focus on the contents and you will become a master
focus on the pot and you will be misguided.
Your eyes only see the body
while the spiritual eye perceives the soul.

"Where is my master?"
"He wanders aimlessly."
"I am his friend; give me a clue
where I may find him."
"Look by the garden stream for he
has fallen in love with the gardener."

Lovers are hopeless, absorbed
in the quest for their loved one.
Can fish survive on dry land?
Would snow not melt if in love with the sun?
Would copper not turn into gold
in the hands of the Alchemist?
A lover cannot linger for long
in the world of color and scent.
You may wander aimlessly, but in the end
you too will be dragged before the King
so why not come now of your own accord?
I am closing the door of speech and opening
a secret way to the world of silence.

False words disturb the heart
only truth brings peace.
False words are like straw stuck in the mouth
that the heart tries desperately to spit out.

A true lover is like a lute
it makes music only when empty
as soon as it is filled the bard lays it down.
If you are full of yourself, you cannot
feel the sweet touch of His fingers.
Empty yourself and surrender
so "here" becomes intoxicated
with the wine of "nowhere."

The Beloved holds my heart as a pen
writing whatever He fancies.
He trims the pen each day for a task
sometimes He smothers it in ink
sometimes He flips it upside down
sometimes He splits the tip for his purpose.
Like a doctor, He knows what is best for the patient.
With one line He wipes clean the entire world
with another He protects it from disaster.

The heart is both aware and unconscious
it has no judgment so it surrenders
to the Beloved's hand that holds it.
Praise the heart that has become aware!
I may call my heart a pen but nothing can explain
this form without form, restrained
yet with free will, a union of paradox.

Beauty is the Garden
scent of roses, murmuring water
flowing gently...
Can words describe the indescribable?

One day you will see me sprawled in the tavern
my turban pawned, my prayer rug stained with wine.
Intoxicated with the teasing kiss of my beloved
I see his curls dancing on the palm of my hand.
Rested, he is tempting me to stay awake
and feast with him till dawn.
How blessed I am that this charmer
entices my spirit away from this world.

Separation bends the back of hope
cruelty ties the hands of longing
yet the lover never despairs.
For a committed heart
everything is possible.

The minstrel is the intimate companion
of the intoxicated lover, he is his strength
and sustenance; his ecstatic songs lead
the lover to the tavern.
But the minstrel who brings God's wine
to the lover is different from the sensual one
whose wine only inflames the body.
The wine the mystics speak of
is not the kind common to man.
The minstrel marks the beginning
of the lover's path, the tavern marks the end.
As the minstrel and the lover become intoxicated
the instigator and the follower become one.
When joy and sorrow dissolve in each other
the minstrel awakens and begins to sing,
"Hand me the cup, Beloved, no wonder I cannot see You
You are my face and closeness is a mystifying veil.
You are my reason, no wonder I cannot see You,
because of the intricate complexity of thought.
You are nearer to me than my jugular vein yet I pretend
to call You from afar so that the jealous ones do not notice
who is sitting beside me."

You have become as hard as rock.
What can rock do to a heart of glass but
shatter it to pieces?
You laugh as dawn laughs at the stars
surrendering their lives.
You burst open the door of my heart and
all thoughts escaped, my patience, defeated,
followed in haste.
With reason and patience gone nothing is left
except mad passion, feverish and weeping,
singing ecstatic songs.
Love is the call and poetry the voice
but I will speak no more for on the subject of love
words shatter.

My heart twisted with passion
in the fire of your words.
Now I see what I saw as fire was only ice
what I saw as water, only a mirage
and our story, an old forgotten dream.

When a true lover appears
calamities blaze up.
I like a heart that can stir the seven seas
fearlessly withstanding the waves.
I like a lover with a fiery heart
burning even hell to ashes.
I like a heart that can wrap the universe
around its hand, catching the eternal light
hanging it like an icicle.
I like a lover with a heart as large as the world
who fights like a lion, not only with others
but with himself, a lover who shatters
the veils of all hearts with the blazing light of Truth.

Love is an attribute of God wanting nothing
repentance is an attribute of man, it is a worm
to Love's dragon, absurd in Love's presence.
Love for anything but Him is unreal
for that which is not Him is a gilded object
shining outside yet empty inside,
light and golden on the outside yet dark within.
The moment divine light disappears
darkness is revealed and unreal love
is extinguished like a candle,
the body is discarded and beauty returns to its source.
The moonlight goes back to the moon
and its reflection disappears from the black wall.
Divine Love is the Sun of Perfection
the Divine Word is its Light
and the creatures are its shadow.

Spring, your luminous face
resembles the face of the Friend
have you borrowed it from Him?
You are a feast for the eyes
yet your essence is hidden
like that of the soul.
The trials of winter are over
beautiful rose, lift your head and smile
the thunder has announced the arrival of spring.
The lily urges her young buds
to open their eyes and behold
the splendor of the Garden.
Stirred by the wind that carries
the sweet scent of union
the branches dance in celebration.

My cup has broken at a flaw.
In the gathering of lovers
there is no place for such a cup.
But I will not mourn this broken body
for the Wine-Bearer has another for me
filled with the pure wine of Spirit.

Following you, I threw
my heart to the winds.
One day your scent filled the air
my heart swelled in gratitude
and scattered in the wind.

A strange illness has befallen my friend!
Sighing and moaning all night
he bashes his head against the wall.
There are no visible symptoms
no fever, no headache.
The doctor taking his pulse declared
his illness not ordinary but caused
by the state of his heart.
My friend refuses food and drink
could it be that the medicine he needs is love?
Lord, please have mercy, cure him of his misery.

"Potions and spells are no cure for a true lover.
If you do not recognize the symptoms
you will never know true Love."

The Beloved gives to each one accordingly.
While I enjoy His pure wine you are drinking vinegar.
Sweetness is the essence of sugar
no amount of wishing turns it sour.
If you want to be a preacher, go and preach
but I am God's musician and play only His music.
He has given me no other sorrow but to seek rhymes
for His poems. Now He has freed me even from that.
So take this poem and tear it to pieces
for meaning is far beyond the whirlwind of words.

To be a dervish and to be in love
is to be the king of the world.
The sorrow of love is a hidden treasure.
I ruined the house of my heart
with my own hands because I knew
the treasure lies hidden in me being ruined.

Love chose me from among all others
it came rushing and brushed against my cheek.
What grace!
The Alchemist reached out from the gold mine
and touched my face.

If I seem full of pride it is because
of the breath He breathed into me.
The jealous moon pulled a veil from
the blue dome of the sky over my face.

The wine kept flowing but no cups were visible
the kisses kept coming but there were no lips.
By the light of that moon the dark night
became as bright as day.

In a dream last night I sought the prayer-niche
in the house of God. A house you need no torch
to find at night for it is the very source of Light,
the nourishment of Spirit.
But could the soul endure that house of Light where
the floors are carpeted by knowledge and wisdom
where Sufis, ecstatic, live bewildered and silent?

My heart, fly like a bird toward that garden of beauty
that safe haven beyond the stark desert of the body!
Enter into the garden of the heart where
you will find roses, pure wine, and music.
In your borrowed body a precious gift is hidden
search for it not only when in pain
learn to love before death claims you.

Do not be seduced by the beauty of calligraphy
learn instead the script of love that will lead you
to the door of the Beloved.
Be drunk on love and you will find the courage
to dive into its endless sea.

Put your thoughts to sleep
let them not cast a shadow
over the moon of your heart.
Drown them in the sea of love.

Under Your steps beloved violets and jasmine trail.
You breathe on a lump of earth and a dove
soars to the sky.
You wash Your hands and the water becomes as gold.
A thorn catches Your robe and it turns into a lute.
Those whom You break become wiser
with one glance You free the wretched from their misery.
Your breath revives all hearts but
I better be silent so You may speak.

The night is dark only for the estranged ones
my night, lit by my Beloved's face is as bright as day.
The whole world may be choked by thorns
but I am wrapped in roses. The whole world
may lie in ruins but my heart sings ecstatically.
The news in the world may be sad and weary
my news is that there is no news at all.

Your beautiful face is the light of my heart
Your gentleness has given me wings
Your laughter is my sacred feast.
Intoxicated by Your delicate scent
my heart can beat for no other.
I walk buoyantly in Your court
and rest in the shade of Your curls.
Immersed in the bliss of Your sea
I surrender at Your feet.
I have become You.

Tell me, my friend, what is greater
the luminous moon, the luscious garden
or the One who created them?
Is a brilliant mind greater
than the One who conceived it?
Even Love that exalts the world becomes
as pliant as wax in His hands.
When I feel my feathers burning
He is opening my wings.
When I feel a dagger piercing my heart
He is protecting me with His shield.
I am lost in awe of Him!

A spark from a burning heart
the sigh of a broken heart
always reach the Beloved.

The dawn of Glory has come spreading its light
and the bird of my soul bursts with song.
In the radiant sun the dust of my body settles
and the Beloved comes to sit at my side.
Touched by His grace my forlorn heart
stirs joyously and begins to dance.
The one whose back has been bent
by the journey springs back to life.
The heart is the light of the world
and the soul its brilliance.
One sets the beat for the other to dance.

When you bury your secret deep in your heart
your wish will come through more quickly.
The secret of seeds buried in the ground
manifest in the flourishing garden.
If gold and silver were not hidden
how could they age in the mine?

No loving heart shuts suddenly without reason.
Sit by its door and keep vigil till dawn
the secret lover appears by night.
Only a heart free from the world's ties
can behold the vision of the Beloved.
And at the moment of union
like a king with an invisible crown
the heart will dance ecstatically
turning the stones into jewels under feet.
But be silent, this precious secret
is not for unworthy ears.

In love, ask for madness
give up reasoning, give up life
look for dangerous adventures
in deserts filled with blood and fire!

Shams, you have been graced with eternal light
look kindly on everyone like the sun and burn
the sorrows of our hearts.
Come like spring reviving the withered plants
and melt our frozen hearts.
Open our lips to a prayer to quench
the longing for your eternal wine.

The infinite green Garden of Love
has many fruits beyond joy and sorrow.
Love is forever green without spring
without autumn.

Come and join the lovers, we will
open the gates to the Garden of Love.
Take refuge in the shade of our home
for we are the neighbors of the sun.
We may be invisible like the soul
and signless like love, yet we are with you
at all times. Do not try to define us
for we are above all concepts.
You are like a stream, imprisoned underground
join and flow with us toward the sea.
We have gambled everything and
reached the state of absolute emptiness.
Knowing that we do not know
now we sing the songs of not-knowing.

Oh heart, fly, you are the phoenix of union!
No one recognizes you, no human no angel
yet you steal and lure thousands of hearts.
For a while you mingle with the world but soon
you spread your wings and fly to the unseen.
Spirit cannot find you, yet you are its feathers and wings.
Eyes cannot see you, yet you are the source of all sight.
Would copper not turn into gold
in the presence of the Alchemist?
Would the seeds not grow in spring?
Would wisdom and knowledge not turn pale
like distant stars in the light of your sun?

You are the summer that melts the world's ice and snow.
Can anyone survive your fiery presence?
Your glance has annihilated hundreds like me.

Sitting under a tree in a beautiful garden
a Sufi, head upon his knee, eyes closed
was lost in contemplation.
A passer-by, annoyed by his state,
could not contain himself,
"How can you sleep? Pay attention
to the signs of God that surround you."
The Sufi calmly answered,
"God's signs I behold within my heart!"

One page of our book will bewilder you forever.
One real moment at the feet of the heart
will turn you from teachers into disciples.

I hide my laughter within and pretend
to be angry, for mixing with those
who are bitter may cause a war,
instead I shed tears for them.
In the vast city of my body, grief is on one side,
I on the other, water on one side, I on the other.
With the bitter I am bitter with the sweet I am sweet.
Hundreds like me are dancing, drunk in His garden
I am tickled by joy and bursting with laughter
my path is joyful and smooth. My heart blossomed
in His garden, dancing and singing praise.
Patience tells me, "I bring news of union."
Gratitude says, "I enrich the heart."
Reason, "I shrink in fear of Him."
Love, "I am the magic."
Spirit says, "I am the foundation of His house."
Ignorance says, "I have no knowledge of Him."
Wisdom: "I owe my mastery to Him."
Abstinence says, "I am His confidante."
Selflessness, "I have surrendered to Him."

There are hundreds of religious books
yet they are all one chapter,
there are a hundred different holy places
yet only one altar.
All roads lead to the one House
from one seed a thousand ears of corn emerge.
There are many kinds of food and drink
with one purpose only, to feed.
The eyes of hunger are greedy,
when satiated with one kind of food
all others become repulsive to your heart.

Where are you rushing drunken heart?
"Hush! It is running toward me!"
Why run aimlessly outside when
I hear your voice from within?
"The heart is often confused, fighting wars,
causing suffering and pain, yet
it is a treasure belonging to me.
Follow that precious heart wherever it goes
it is a prayer rising to the sky
the milk in the breast of the clouds
the whirling wind in the garden.
It has neither face nor form, yet
it gives meaning to the world
it has neither head nor feet, yet
it is the world's head and feet.

It is a flame that illuminates the body
without which it will perish.
Eternal and magic it rules the universe,
spills the blood of kings, creates turmoil,
mixes with everyone, yet it is always alone."

Happy is the moment when with compassion
you caress the lover's head.
Happy is the moment when the breeze
of spring arises from the depths of autumn.

Happy is the moment when with a cup of wine
the Beloved invites you to the gathering,
that immortal wine makes every atom rejoice.

Happy is the moment when the Beloved
demands a promise and sweetly accepts your pledge.

Happy is the moment when the heart says,
"I have not yet planted my garden."
and you reply, "Whatever you plant shall grow."

Happy is the moment when separation
bids you, "Good night."

Happy is the moment when dawn
greets you, "Good morning."

Happy is the moment when Love
wrapped in the cloud of divine grace
rains pearls upon the desert.

Part Three

Garden of Spirit

I call God's infinite Grace a garden, for it is the source
of all generosity and beauty, the essence of all gardens.
How else could I describe that which eyes cannot behold?
Was not the Divine Light called "a lamp"?
These are not comparisons but allegories so those who
become bewildered may catch a glimpse of Reality.

With every breath, from left and right, the voice
of Love is calling. What else are we seeking?
Friends, let us gather our belongings,
leave this dusty world, and return to our home
where we were once companions of angels
and where in the end we shall all return.

We are higher than the heavens and greater
than the angels. Our true home is Divine Majesty.
Could the glory of the Beloved be compared
with the world of dust? Fortunate is the one
who surrenders to Him, whose sweet scent is carried
on the breeze, and who's light can split the moon.

Friends, let us return to the source of pure essence
that nothing else can equal. Remember,
we are pearls in the ocean of Spirit. If not, why are
these constant waves surging through our hearts?
The primeval wave created the vessel of this body,
as it breaks we will be united with the Friend.

As candlelight is absorbed in the rays of the sun
as the rivers are absorbed in the sea
so the lover melts into the Beloved.
Until the lover is consumed completely by longing
the Beloved's face remains hidden.

Your benevolence has no rival!
Every door is shut except Yours
so a stranger lost at night
finds no other door but Yours.

Only in the pure air of selflessness the heart can fly
only in the kingdom of selflessness the spirit can soar.
May God's light shine upon all lovers so they find
shelter in the shade of selflessness.
You may offer a thousand fortunes to a lover
still he will choose selflessness in the end.
Look at me, I threw myself into adversity
and found such sweetness in being selfless!
At the feet of selflessness superiority becomes redundant.
My friend, do not spend time with gloomy people
let not the dust of their sadness spoil your joy.
Empty your house of yourself and
invite the Beloved as a guest.

All are satellites around You, the suns
and planets have entered Your orbit.
Beloved, am I the seeker or the sought?
Until I am I, You are another.
There is no place for "You" and "I" in unity.

Let no feet remain that lead us to thorns
let no heads remain that lead us to denial.
There is water flowing in the middle of the stream
and water frozen on the banks
one is swift, the other stagnant.
Be aware, swift one, or you too may freeze.
It is the sun that transforms stones into gems,
it is the sun of eternal love shining in your heart
that stirs it into service and leads it to mastery.
The king covers the falcon's eyes so it can detach
from its own kind and gaze only at his face.
Misguided is the one who takes his gaze
off the Beloved and turns toward another.
A fool gives up Christ to buy a donkey
the wise man sells his donkey to follow Christ.

Seek the light beyond the light of day and night
beyond judgment, the light bestowed by God.
Leaving the darkness we are the moonlight
returning to the moon, for the truth is
To Him we shall all return.

My thoughts spin in a whirlwind of passion
my heart circles in the air like a bird in flight
every atom of my being is whirling.
Is my Beloved whirling everywhere too?

Spring is here
we will not leave this garden and the tall cypress.
Take off your mask and close the door
it is only you and I in this empty house.
Today we are the special companions of love
holding the cup-of-no-concern in our hands.
Sweet minstrel, play the most enchanting melody
cup-bearer, bring the wine quickly so
we may drink happily and sleep contented
in the shade of eternal grace.
This wine does not pass through the lips
this sleep is not brought by the night.
Oh heart, the moment you dissolve completely
in that eternal wine you will attain perfection.
Today is a day of such happiness, such glory
a day not lit by the sun but by the Original Light
where you abide hidden in Eternity.

But I better be silent for words manifest thoughts
and thoughts not watered by Spirit become
dry and empty very quickly.

Once again music fills the air
my soul opens its arms
and invites my heart to dance.
The world is smiling, wrapped in a luminous glow
the table is set, the guest has arrived
the scent of spring over the green meadows
is overwhelming and I am drunk with love.
The Beloved is the whole ocean, I
a curl of mist on its surface.
He is a precious treasure
I am a speck of dust, no one.
Yet, forgive my boasting,
I can split the moon in two
with the light of my Beloved
for I am wild with love!

At night, drifting like the wind
I pace sleepless through the town.
Sober people focus on the practical
but I cannot be sensible
ruined and drunk as I am on love.

Worldly goods and your body are like snow
melting into nothing, but to you
the snow seems better because you doubt.
Your precious opinions thirsting for certainty
cannot fly to the Garden of Truth.
As opinion acquires knowledge and progresses further
it begins to emanate the scent of certainty.
Fancy is born of opinion,
vision and intuition from certainty.

Since I tasted the sweetness of the Beloved
I became a seer, my feet do not tremble,
I do not walk like the blind,
I step boldly toward my spiritual home.
What the Beloved whispered to the rose
making her blossom, He said to my heart
and made it a hundred times
more beautiful.

Open the gates of Grace, Beloved!
You, the Soul of all souls and dweller
of a thousand worlds, cut the neck
of separation with your ageless sword.

At last Your glorious sun shines, bestowing
the glow of youth upon this ancient world.
What celebration for the soul, what joy!
The wine is pouring, sounds of lute and
tambourine are rising in the air, the rose garden
is full with the songs of the nightingale.
In the midst of the flowering branches
the lovers each holding a cup
shout and cheer, lost to themselves
unable to tell the cup from the wine.
Please, send my greetings to the lovers if you
can find one sober enough to deliver this message.

Love rushed into my veins
emptying me of myself.
Now filled with the Beloved
my only possession is my name.

Last night I dreamed myself as empty of self
and fainted from the glory.
The beauty and grace of emptiness
intoxicated me till dawn.
I saw this precious poverty as a mine of ruby
and its hue enfolded me in red silk.
I heard cries, "Drink, drink now!"
from the ecstatic circle of lovers and
felt the ring of the Beloved on my ear.
A thousand voices shouted from the surging
sea of Spirit and my soul rose in ecstasy.

If you only knew what bliss I found in being nothing
you would not advise me how to live.
When the sword of nothingness ends my life
I will laugh at those who mourn my death.

Today my estranged lover has returned.
Faithful friends, come and dance with joy
my treasure has come home.
Eyes, behold the garden, ears, gather
the intoxicating words coming from
the lips of my enchanting lover!
Today the eternal wine flows freely
I will throw all caution to the wind.
I am a hunting falcon, no longer in captivity.
My heart has lost all patience
it will no longer listen to your stories.
I am a seed scattered from the barn of heaven
when spring comes rushing in my heart
I will burst in green.
Winter seems now a long forgotten dream.

When I start on the path He is my guide
when I look for love He is my enchanter.
When I fight a war He is my dagger
when I seek peace He is my ambassador.
At the feast He is my wine and my sweets
in the garden He is the scent of jasmine.
In the mine He is the ruby
in the sea He is the pearl.
In the desert He is the oasis
in the heavenly spheres He is a star.
When I seek patience He is my ultimate Master
when I burn in grief He is the censer.
When I write He is my pen and paper
when I chase after a rhyme He is my inspiration.
When I wake up He is my awareness
when I go to sleep He haunts my dreams.
His perfection is beyond grasp, no pen or brush
could ever describe Him. Throw your learning
let Him become your book.

Today, amazed and bewildered,
I closed the door to thought
and turned to music.
There are a hundred ways to kneel
and pray at the altar of the Beloved.

Are You Sun, Venus, or Moon?
I know not.
What do You want from your bewildered madman?
I know not.
Which plains do You inhabit
in perfect grace and harmony?
I know not.
You made my spirit blossom like a rose
Your face illuminated mine, who are You?
I know not.
You are a boundless sea
full of treasures I have never known
who are You?
I know not.
You are the infinite Sun, the light of God's essence
are You God?
I know not.
But I must stop, talking only creates confusion
intoxicated by You, I no longer know
if I am drunk or sober!

I speak of Spring but not
of the season of spring.
I speak of drunkenness but not
of the one caused by wine.
I talk of branches dancing in the wind
but what I mean is the breath of God.

There are stars beyond the visible stars where
there is no risk of burning up or colliding
where astral travelers wander in other heavens
besides the seven that we know.
Those stars have inherited the shining light of God
and are neither joined nor separate from each other.
Souls whose rising sign derives from those stars
are like meteors burning all that stands in their path.
Held between the two fingers of God, they emanate light
that is unaffected by disharmony and darkness.
Although God scatters light upon all souls, only the souls
who are aware are fortunate enough to have held up
their robes to receive it and have turned their face
from anything but God. Those unaware of the robe
of love end up without a share of that scattering of light.

You enter in the heart and it begins
to glow like Mount Sinai.
You enter into any home and
illuminate it with Your brightness.
You are the wine at every feast
causing uproar and excitement.
When all joy and passion have gone
from this weary world
You bring it back to life
revealing the wondrous worlds beyond.
What a marvel! You, the source of light,
circling around the earth all day and night,
a Heavenly King serving a slave.
A beggar asks the king for alms, but
what could a king beg for from a beggar?
Nothing happens by chance
no one goes on a quest without a reason
without the pull of the magnet
there is no action.

My words are food for the angels
they complain when I am silent.
Not being one of them, what do you know
of angel's food or what is cooking
in the kitchen of thought whose Chef is God?

A seeker of Truth looks beyond the apparent
and contemplates the hidden. What the senses perceive
is only a distortion. We all look for something
that is not yet in existence, beggars look for coins,
shopkeepers for profit, farmers for harvest, pupils
for knowledge, and seekers for enlightenment.
Non-existence is the treasure house of God
in the process of becoming manifest.

The icy winds, the scorching heat, the storms,
the clouds, and the lightening all exist in order to make
the differences apparent so the Earth may reveal
the gems she has stolen from the Treasury of the Almighty.
God's kindness is revealed in spring, His wrath in autumn
winter is the allegory of crucifixion exposing the thief
hidden in you. As the body is the denier of the light of Spirit
God sends it trials of suffering and pain so the gold
of the Spirit may manifest.

Surrender, if you are a seeker of union
find your place in the heart of nothingness.
While still in the cage of your being
behold the spirit bird before it flies away.
Since you were once drunk on eternity
pick up the sword of now and strike the ego.
Remove the dregs of separation, become pure
so the cup of true reality can be filled
with the pure wine of Spirit.

As long as you are crawling like a snake on this earth
do not hope to swim like fish in the sea of Spirit.
If you seek the kinship of nothingness, pick up
the broom of no and sweep all illusions.
If you want to journey, climb the mount of meaning
if you settle, settle only in the green dome of heaven.
Strive constantly, always be thirsty, no matter what
heights you have reached, keep going higher.
A spirit with an aim is always facing the door
lift your head and fly alone toward the light
for the body only casts long dark shadows.
Be the blazing fire and the one who burns
be the wine and the one who drinks
and be intoxicated with neither.

Beyond belief and disbelief
lies the vast expanse of ecstasy
where the mystic lays his head
on the cushion of Truth.

You have been caught in the claws of a lion
my friend, do not look for happiness.
Only harshness can defeat the hidden enemy inside you.
A man beating a rug with a stick does not
aim at the rug but at the dust inside it.
Your ego is covered with many dusty veils
you cannot remove them at once.
With each blow, little by little
they will disappear from the face of your heart.
But do not try to escape into sleep
the Beloved's sharp claws will chase you in your dreams.
A carpenter does not carve a piece of wood out of cruelty
but in order to create a beautiful shape.
The harsh hand of the Beloved is a blessing, my friend,
it will refine you and make you pure in the end.

The lover's concern is passion and madness
the charming game the Beloved plays is aloof detachment.
Learn the dance of light from the atoms
learn to jump into the fire like the moth.
Learn to charge like a lion, not sneak like a fox.
Learn to soar like a falcon, not flutter
from flower to flower like a butterfly.
Spring water tastes sweet but is incomparable
to the majesty of the ocean.
Your being is the cup that holds all secrets
do not let them leak through your eyes and ears.

What are you looking for, my friend,
completely absorbed in the affairs of this world?
Unless you strive for Spirit your bread will remain
unbaked and your destiny unfulfilled.
Do not waste your life decorating your gravestone.
Instead dig a grave and bury your ego, surrender to Him
so His breath may replenish your being.

In the mirror of my soul, my love,
I see now only your luminous face
my soul and yours are one.
My mind was the master of my house once
now it is only your servant.
My spirit was love-struck from the start
though a bit concerned by your earthly form.
And now that the mud has settled and
my clarity has returned
this you and I is no more!

Being self-absorbed
you are far from me even in my presence.
Cease to be, for on the path of love
it is either you or me.

A Master enters life in silence
His message is heard only in silence.

Drink His precious wine and forget yourself
do not demean the greatness of His love.
He turns the wheel of heaven, He is the helper
of those who suffer in silence.

Follow Him without a word, He knows
your every deed and will reveal one by one
the thoughts buried in your heart. He will
turn them into birds and set them free, in silence.

To glimpse the splendor of that moon
turn your eyes inward, talk not
of this world or of the next
let Him pull you toward oneness
in silence.

I felt your anguish and your deep sighs last night.
I will not let you wait anymore. I will take you
to the secret path of union so you
may be delivered from the whirlpool of Time.
But the delight and joy that awaits you at the end
is in proportion to the pain endured on the journey.
It is exile that makes the joy of homecoming greater.

There is a loneliness more precious than life
there is a freedom more precious than the world.
Infinitely more precious than life and the world
is that moment when one is alone with God.

"Wherever you turn there is His face."
Those graced with clear vision see
the signs of the Creator everywhere.
For them all things, be it plant or animal,
become a contemplation of Divine beauty.
The annihilated lovers see the Beloved's face
even in the water they drink while
others only see their own reflection.

Do not ask why my heart is bleeding
why my face is pale
just walk away without saying a word.
Yesterday you knocked on the door of my heart
"Open the door but be silent!"
I gasped biting my hand lest my cry escape.
"Why do you complain? You are my flute
until I play you, do not speak of pain."
But why are you torturing me?
"Be silent and follow me without a word."
Why do you get angry when I am silent
and order me to speak? He smiled sweetly,
"Come with me and I will show you.
What you see as burning fire
is really a luscious garden."
Suddenly the fire transformed into a rose
and whispered,
"If you must speak, speak only of
my Beloved's loving kindness."

Seek love, seek love!
It is the diamond of your being.
Seek the One, seek the One!
He is yours for eternity
but do not call Him yours for what is yours
is only sorrow and longing.

Who would write on a page already filled with writings?
Who would plant a sapling where one is already planted?
One would look for an empty page and virgin soil.
Become bare like the earth so the Beloved
may plant His seed, become a blank page
so His pen may write upon you.

Those who conquer their ego before death
become mentors of the angels and protectors
of the poor. They have glimpsed Spirit
and know how to live.

Shams, what road you took departing
by which secret way did you return?
Was it the same the souls take each night
leaving behind a town of empty cages?
A bird with tied wings cannot fly
only a soul free from attachments
can reach the higher planes from where
the truth can be seen.

But let us not disturb the silence
with the hollow drum of words.

By continuous remembrance of God
man, illuminated by the light of Truth
advances toward his perfect essence
that wondrous sea where each wave
breaks with the sound, "I am the Truth!"

The ego is a ladder that we climb
and from which we all fall in the end.
The higher the ego climbs, the more
devastating will be the fall.
In its foolishness the inflated ego
claims equality with God.
Die to yourself and live through Him
if you are seeking Unity.
Aiming to reign with God is very far
from being in God.

Play for love, my glorious musician
keep playing your inspiring tunes, do not stop.
You are my only friend, the solace of my soul
do not leave now that my heart has fallen in love
feeling so tender and open to pain.

Unlike man's sorrows that taste bitter
Love's pain is sweet, do not avoid it
for if it leaves you even for a moment
your heart will turn into a tomb and
you into a mourner.
Embrace the pain of Love,
let it be your comfort
and the sorrows of the night will end.

My sweet idol, what was that drink last night?
I want the same for the rest of my life.
I had no thirst for wine until I saw your face
reflected in the glass you placed in my hand.

Now, desolate and gloomy like the night
I am covered with the black veil of separation.
Oh how I long to see your face and glow again
like the earth in the bright morning sun.
You left in haste, my heart is out of control.
Come back, my love and nurture me like you
nurture the heavens and the earth.
I tell my heart, "Suffer in silence
and do not complain!"
but it has become deaf.

I blossomed in His spring,
I drank wine in His abundant garden
and dissolved in the beauty of His face.

A man who has prospered in foreign lands
soon forgets his hometown. No wonder
his spirit too does not remember
the ancient abode of its birthplace.
Like sleep, the world has covered it
as clouds cover the stars.
He has walked in many cities but never swept
the dust from his spiritual eyes nor made
any effort to purify his heart
to see through the aperture of mystery
the whole picture with clarity.

Where is my wise musician who plays
only for love ignoring all other requests?
Hoping to see him I have grown old and weary
and may have to take my wish to my grave.
If you see him wandering alone on the seashore
please convey to him my longing and tears.
Only the love of a passionate heart might draw him near.

I drank Your nectar, Beloved,
and grew in majesty. Now
emanating Your sweet fragrance
even the angel of death has no hope.

Be warned lover, intoxicated with the wine of love
you are unaware that you are on the edge of the roof,
sit down or descend. Each delightful moment
you enjoy with the Beloved is as if you are
perched on the edge of the roof.
Be on guard, tremble over it as for a treasure
for disaster may come suddenly. You may
not see the edge but the Spirit does and fears that
your unawareness signals the start of your descent.
Take warning from the people of Noah and Lot
for all sudden shocks, calamities, and deaths
occur on the edge of the roof of enjoyment.

I wonder, Spirit, since you live in this world
why the dust does not praise you,
why poison still tastes bitter?
Why this anger, violence, why this unawareness?
One day in your garden I wondered why
in your presence, a thorn remains a thorn?
Has God masked your face to keep you hidden
or is it that the very eye of the world is so coarse
that it is unable to behold the gentleness of your face?

There is another language beyond language
another place beyond heaven and hell.
Precious gems come from another mine
the heart draws light from another source.

How much joy and pain each part of your body has
experienced since emerging from non-existence!
Each part has its own story to tell, holding in its memory
the gifts of the Provider hidden in the pages of Time.

As ice in summer tells the story of winter's cold winds,
as fruit in winter tells the story of the sun's embrace,
so are the stories of those living in union pregnant
with the wonders of the invisible. They have withdrawn
their eyes from the world, living in ecstasy
covered by an invisible veil. They are the witnesses
of the creation of life and the mystery of union.

He who is not captured by Love
is like a wingless bird.
What understanding can he have of the world
without knowing the Knower?
In love with himself, he is easily lured astray
with no courage to embark on the path.
The Beloved is the guardian of the gate
that only He can open.
Those unable to pass are robbed of their essence.
Dawn may come, but they remain asleep,
while in our sky, the sun never sets nor rises.

You smile so charmingly
what secret do you hide in your heart?
You laugh fresh as the dawn
where did you spend last night?
You have set everything on fire and
now sit in the midst of flames, laughing.
You returned from God's tavern, drunk
and joyful, laughing at good and evil.
You appear as the essence of laughter.
All trees wither in autumn, you laugh
fresh as a rose. What enchanted garden
do you come from? You are certainty
laughing at opinion and pretence,
you are contemplation laughing at
accumulated knowledge.
You laugh at the path, the traveler,
and the journey.
Before the everlasting presence
you are the witness and the witnessed!

Swaying between joy and sorrow
you are the prey of the transient.
Love's infinite garden holds other fruit
besides laughter and tears
forever fresh and green without
spring without autumn.

Master your vicious ego and judgmental mind
then with clear purpose, silent and alone
you can start on your journey toward Spirit.
The moon will light the signs on your path
and lead you toward the place with no signs.
The beautiful names of God you have repeated enough
now enter the stage of knowing their essence.
No longer a seeker, you have arrived at the threshold
of the Divine. Now servant and king, apparent
and hidden, you have become silent as Spirit.

Green worlds, green gardens
roses smiling, rubies aflame
souls uniting one with another
revealing the greatness of Beauty.

Night has shattered my understanding and my senses
no hope is left, no fear, no despair.
God has taken me in the Sea of Mercy.
I do not know with what skills He will fill me
and send me back to the world.
Some He bestows with the light of His majesty
others with vain fantasies.
If I had any judgment and skill of my own
my decision and foresight would be under my control.
At night my awareness and senses
would not leave without my knowing.
I should be aware of the stages of my soul's journey
both at the time of sleep and at the time of trouble.
But since the power to free or bind is His
I am left with empty hands and wonder
from whom comes this self-conceit of mine?
When unconscious, I am nothing
when conscious, I am in torment.
Truly the state of possessing nothing suits me better
since all troubles arise from imagining
that I posses something.
So, I will just stand naked and in tears at His gate
blinded by my weeping.

I shape these poems, You give them spirit
but no, I am wrong, both come from You.
Be glorified in heaven and on earth forever
so people can become one in heart,
one in aim, and one with the Divine.
Let separation and duality disappear
for real existence is only in unity.
In the moment of recognition, our spirits
will remember being one from the beginning.

I stole a glance from You and my eyes
became longing and wistful.
I heard one word from Your lips and
my ears deafened to the world.

But my friend, if you have not had this experience
you are excused to be entangled in this world.

I became the sea
and each atom flamed out of me in glory
I became fire
and each moment became an eternity....

At the time of night prayer when the sun has set
as the senses close, the way to the unseen opens.
The angel of sleep, like a shepherd, drives the spirits
to the placeless, to spiritual meadows of a thousand marvels.
As sleep erases the impressions of this world
what cities, what gardens the spirit beholds there!
Remembering no more the burdens
and the weight on this earth
the heart is freed from all the cares of this world.

At dawn a moon appeared in the sky,
slid down, and looked at me.
Then like a hawk hunting a bird
it seized me up and ran across the sky.
When I looked, I saw myself no more
through the grace of that moon
my body had become all soul.
Journeying on as soul, I saw nothing but that moon
until the eternal secret was revealed.
The nine spheres of heaven
were absorbed in that moon,
the ship of my being dissolved in that sea.
That sea surged up, intelligence rose again
forming a voice, the sea foamed and
from each foam-bubble something took form
something sprang clothed in a body.
Then each foam-fleck of body
receiving a sign from the sea melted
immediately becoming Spirit in that sea.
Without the royal fortune of Shams of Tabriz
no one could behold the moon nor become the sea.

Flowing from Spirit, water trails its skirt
purifying the world through Grace.
Becoming polluted, with its virtues spent
it rushes back to the Fountain of Origin.
Then, cleansed and clad in a robe of purity
it flows back to the earth
balm and cure for the tired soul.

The dawn of Grace has come
the eternal Light has come!
It is time for union
time for tolerance and generosity.
Is this the face of the ancient King
of wisdom or just a veil?
You may answer, but be aware
you posses two heads
one earthly and one heavenly.
Focus on the one able to perceive
the infinite worlds hidden
beyond the apparent.
Wine-Bearer, keep pouring the wine
even though the cup of our understanding
is too narrow for the truth.

The illusion we have created of this world
serves only the desires of our mind.
The essence of our being is nothingness.
From behind the veils
the One watches over our being
while in the world we are only shadows.

Come near, come near!
Since you are me and I am you
there is no more separation.
We are Light upon Light
why this conflict, this stubbornness?
What light flees from such a Light?
We are all one complete being, why this double vision?
Why do the rich look at the poor with distaste?
Why does the right hand look upon the left with disgust?
Since both are part of you, what is good about the right
what is distasteful about the left?
We are entirely one essence, one intellect, and one head
yet we see double because of our misconceptions.
How much longer will you drag this baggage
of the five senses and the six directions?
Draw near to Unity!
Rise above your selfishness and merge with all!
On your own, you are only a seed of grain
but together with all, you are a gold mine.
Know that the spirit is one but bodies are countless
just as almonds share the same quality of being oily.
The meaning of a word is the same in different languages
the water becomes one once the cups are broken.
Spirit sends news to everyone with vision
for in Unity the heart is free from the bondage of words.

At last you left, departed into the unseen.
I wonder, I wonder what route
you took leaving this world?
You broke the cage with your wings
and flew to the world of Spirit.

You were a falcon captured by an old crone
but when you heard the King's drum
you flew to the place of placelessness.
You were a drunken nightingale among owls
but His sweet scent drew you to His rose garden.
You suffered a hangover from bad wine but at last
you found your way to the eternal tavern.

You left the bow like an arrow aiming
straight at the target of bliss.
You ignored the false signs of the world
and flew to the place of no signs.

Oh heart, what a rare bird you are, on your wings
of fear and hope, as a shield you went straight
for the spear. The rose fears autumn but you
braved the cruel autumn winds.
Rest now safely, in the loving arms of the Beloved.

Look in my eyes and you will see
God's Beauty and Truth.
God sees His Beauty reflected in us
but do not speak of this secret
for He will spill your blood.

Blessed is the moment when we sit in the garden
You and I.
Two forms, two faces, but a single soul
You and I.
The birds will sing songs of eternal life
the moment we enter into the rose garden
You and I.
The stars of heaven will come to look at us
beautiful as the moon, entwined in ecstasy
You and I.
The birds of paradise will be filled with envy
when they hear us laughing happily
You and I.
What a marvel, us sitting here together
and at the same time in Iraq and Khorasan
You and I.
One form on this earth and in Eternity
You and I.

I dissolved as a grain of salt
in your Sea of Serenity.
Nothing remained, no faith,
no certainty, no doubt.
In my heart a star was born
and inside all worlds dissolved.

Index of First Lines

Legend for poems

> D = Divan of Shams
>
> M [I, II, III, IV, V, VI] = Masnavi
>
> R = Rubayiat
>
> SK = Shafii Kadkani's Selection of the Divan

Garden of the Soul

Garden of the Heart

Garden of Spirit